BECAUSE YOU ARE MY TEACHER

By Sherry North · Illustrated by Marcellus Hall

SCHOLASTIC INC.

This book features two of Earth's five oceans and all seven of its continents. The five oceans are the Arctic, Atlantic, Indian, Pacific, and Southern. The seven continents are Africa, Antarctica, Asia, Australia, Europe, North America, and South America. Blue whales live in all of the world's oceans, including the North Atlantic; camels and Egyptian pyramids are in Africa; penguins live in Antarctica; howler monkeys and the Amazon River are in South America; the Great Wall of China is in Asia; the deepest, darkest ocean is the Pacific; African elephants live in the grasslands and forests of Africa; the Grand Canyon (in the state of Arizona) is in North America; kangaroos live in Australia; the Everglades (in the state of Florida) are in North America; and the city of Venice (in the country of Italy) is in Europe.

ISBN 978-0-545-76888-7

Text copyright © 2012 by Sherry North.
Illustrations copyright © 2012 by Marcellus Hall. All rights reserved.
Published by Scholastic Inc., 557 Broadway, New York, NY 10012,
by arrangement with Abrams Books for Young Readers,
an imprint of Harry N. Abrams, Inc. SCHOLASTIC and associated
logos are trademarks and/or registered trademarks of Scholastic Inc.

12 11 10 9 8 7 6 5 4 3 2 1   14 15 16 17 18 19/0

Printed in the U.S.A.   40

First Scholastic printing, May 2014

The illustrations in this book were created using watercolor on paper.
Book design by Chad W. Beckerman

For my parents, who taught me to
reach for the stars, and for the teachers
who showed me how
—SN

If we had a schooner, we would have our class at sea

And study the Atlantic, where the great blue whales roam free.

If we had some camels, we would trek through desert lands

To see the ancient pyramids rising from the sands.

If we had a chopper, we would soar above the cone

Of a rumbling volcano as it churns out liquid stone.

If we had sleek ski gear, we would cross Antarctic fields

To find the spot where penguin chicks are eating their first meals.

If we had a river raft, we would tour the Amazon

And listen as the howler monkeys growl their spooky song.

If we had hot-air balloons, we would set out on a quest

To study China's Great Wall from the east end to the west.

If we had swift kayaks, we would plunge through twists and falls, Exploring the Grand Canyon, where the river carves the walls.

If we had hang gliders, we would get a bird's-eye view

Of the Australian outback and the large red kangaroo.

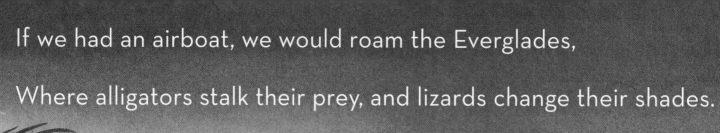

If we had an airboat, we would roam the Everglades,

Where alligators stalk their prey, and lizards change their shades.

If we had a gondola, we would glide beneath the stars

In Venice, where the people ride in boats instead of cars.

If we had a rocket, we would study Earth from space.

With seven sprawling continents, our home is quite a place!

Our classroom is our vessel,

always headed someplace new.

Because you are our teacher,

We'll explore the world with you.